Financial Literacy

11 THINGS THAT EVERYONE NEEDS TO KNOW

By Darby Guillory Jr

Published by 487 Holdings LLC

ISBN 978-1-304-98379-4

For Worldwide Distribution, Printed in the USA

Table of Contents

Opening:

The Freedom of Financial Literacy

Imagine a life where you are no longer bound by the constraints of financial uncertainty. A life where your choices are driven by opportunities, not limitations. This is the profound freedom that financial literacy can bestow upon you—the ability to shape your destiny, make informed decisions, and take charge of your financial well-being.

Introduction: Unshackling the Chains of Financial Uncertainty

Financial literacy is not just about numbers and budgets; it is the key that unlocks the doors to a world of possibilities. It is the passport to a future where your financial choices are guided by knowledge, not guesswork.

Consider this: with financial literacy, you can:

1. **Escape the Cycle of Debt**: Break free from the burden of debt that often holds people captive. Understand the principles of responsible borrowing and debt management to regain control of your financial life.

2. **Build a Secure Future:** Secure your future by saving and investing wisely. Whether it's planning for retirement, purchasing a home, or funding your dreams, financial literacy empowers you to set achievable goals and work towards them.

3. **Protect Your Assets**: Safeguard your hard-earned money from scams, fraud, and financial pitfalls. Recognize red flags and make informed decisions to protect your financial well-being.

4. **Pursue Your Passions**: Have the means to explore your passions and interests without the constraints of financial stress. Whether it's starting a business, traveling the world, or pursuing a creative endeavor, financial literacy can help you make it a reality.

5. **Navigate Life's Challenges**: Face life's inevitable challenges, such as unexpected medical expenses, job loss, or emergencies, with resilience. Financial literacy provides the safety net you need to weather these storms.

6. **Give Back and Make an Impact**: Once you've achieved financial stability, you have the opportunity to make a positive impact on your community and the world. Financial literacy enables you to support causes you believe in and contribute to the greater good.

The freedom of financial literacy extends far beyond just managing your money; it empowers you to design the life you want to live. It allows you to make choices aligned with your values, aspirations, and dreams. It liberates you from the constraints of financial uncertainty and opens doors to a brighter, more promising future.

In the chapters that follow, we will explore the world of financial literacy—its principles, strategies, and real-life applications. We will provide you with the knowledge and tools you need to embark on your journey towards financial freedom. So, embrace the freedom that financial literacy can bring, and let's embark on this transformative journey together.

CHAPTER 1

Budget

Introduction to Budgeting

Welcome to the world of budgeting, where you'll embark on a journey to understand the art of managing your finances. Imagine being in control of your money, ensuring that you can pay your bills, save for your goals, and still enjoy the things you love. That's the power of budgeting. In this chapter, we'll follow the story of Alex, an 18-year-old navigating the financial challenges of adulthood, and discover the importance of budgeting along the way.

Chapter: Alex's Budgeting Adventure

Once upon a time in the bustling city of Financeville, there lived a young adult named Alex. Freshly 18 and eager to embrace the world of independence, Alex was about to face one of life's essential skills: budgeting. It all began when Alex received his first paycheck from his part-time job at the local bookstore.

Excited about his newfound financial freedom, Alex started spending on everything that caught his eye—new clothes, gadgets, eating out with friends, and more. But as the days passed, a harsh reality hit him like a ton of bricks: his bank account was rapidly dwindling, and bills were piling up.

Fun Fact #1: Budgeting helps you control your money and avoid overspending.

Panicking, Alex turned to his wise grandparent, who shared a valuable secret—budgeting. With guidance, Alex learned that budgeting was like creating a plan for his money. It involved tracking his income and expenses, allowing him to see exactly where his hard-earned dollars were going.

Alex decided to give budgeting a try. He started by listing all sources of income, including his part-time job earnings and any allowances he received. Then, he made a list of monthly expenses, which included rent, groceries, utility bills, and, of course, a bit of spending money for fun.

Fun Fact #2: Budgets can help you balance spending on necessities, fun stuff, and savings.

To put his plan into action, Alex used a simple rule: the 50/25/15/10 rule. This rule suggests dividing your income into four categories:

1. **50% for Needs**: This includes things like rent or mortgage, groceries, utilities, and transportation.

2. **25% for Wants**: This is where you allocate money for entertainment, dining out, and other fun activities.

3. **15% for Savings**: Always set aside a portion of your income for future needs or goals, such as emergencies, education, or a dream vacation.

4. **10% for Giving**: Tithing to your church or contributing to charities and foundations you believe in is a meaningful and impactful way to demonstrate your genuine care and concern for God and others.

Alex plugged in the numbers and discovered that he was overspending on his "**wants**" category. He frequently dine out and made impulsive purchases that was causing his budget to spiral out of control.

Fun Fact #3: Budgets can help you spot areas where you're overspending and then make adjustments.

With determination and a newfound sense of responsibility, Alex made some changes. He decided to cook more at home and limit unnecessary spending on items he didn't really need. This not only helped Alex stay within his budget but also reduced the stress of wondering if his could cover their bills.

As the months went by, Alex became a budgeting pro. He watched his savings grow, and with discipline and a clear financial plan, he began saving for a future vacation he had always dreamed of.

Fun Fact #4: Budgeting can help you achieve your financial goals, whether it's a vacation, a new gadget, or college.

Summary: Why Budgeting is Important

Budgeting is a vital financial skill for several reasons:

1. **Control Your Finances**: Budgeting allows you to take control of your money rather than letting it control you. It

helps you avoid overspending and ensures you can cover your needs.

2. **Achieve Financial Goals**: Whether it's saving for a vacation, buying a new gadget, or paying for college, budgeting helps you allocate funds toward your goals.

3. **Emergency Preparedness**: With a budget, you're better prepared for unexpected expenses like medical bills or car repairs. Your emergency fund becomes an essential part of your budget.

4. **Reduce Stress**: Budgeting reduces financial stress. Knowing you can meet your financial commitments brings peace of mind.

5. **Sustainable Living**: It promotes sustainable financial habits by encouraging responsible spending and saving.

Closing Summary

Budgeting is the cornerstone of financial success. It empowers you to take control of your money, prioritize your spending, and work toward your dreams. By following a budget, like Alex did, you can enjoy both your everyday life and your financial future. Remember, budgeting isn't about restricting your fun; it's about making sure your money is working for you, not against you. So, start your budgeting adventure today, and watch your financial goals become a reality!

Chapter 2

Debt

Introduction to Debt

Welcome to the world of debt, a topic that becomes increasingly important as you step into adulthood. Debt can be a powerful tool, but it's essential to understand how to manage it wisely. In this chapter, we'll follow the journey of Emma, an 18-year-old on the verge of making her first significant financial decisions and explore the world of debt together.

Chapter: Emma's Debt Dilemma

Once upon a time in a bustling suburb, Emma, an 18-year-old high school graduate, was eager to embrace the world beyond her hometown. With dreams of attending college and pursuing her passion for photography, she knew she needed money. That's when the topic of debt entered her life.

Emma learned about various types of debt. Some people carried student loans to finance their education, while others used credit cards to make purchases they couldn't afford upfront. It all seemed a bit overwhelming at first.

Fun Fact #1: Debt is money borrowed that you must repay, often with interest.

One day, as Emma was researching student loans, she discovered that not all debt was created equal. Some, like student loans, could be considered "good debt" because they invested in her future by enabling her to pursue a college degree. Others, like credit card debt used for impulsive shopping sprees, were considered "bad debt" because they didn't lead to long-term benefits.

Emma decided to explore the concept further. She knew that borrowing money came with a price—interest. Interest was the extra money you had to pay back on top of the amount you borrowed. Emma realized that the interest rate on debt made a significant difference in how much it would ultimately cost her.

Fun Fact #2: The interest rate on debt affects how much you'll pay back in the end.

To make informed decisions, Emma decided to learn more about credit scores. A credit score was like a report card for her financial behavior. It could affect her ability to borrow money and the interest rates she'd be offered.

Emma discovered that responsible financial habits, like paying bills on time and not maxing out credit cards, helped build a good credit score. A higher credit score meant better terms on loans and credit cards.

Fun Fact #3: Your credit score can open doors to better financial opportunities.

As Emma continued her research, she also learned about the dangers of excessive debt. High levels of debt could lead to stress, limited financial choices, and even damage her credit score if she couldn't make payments on time.

Fun Fact #4: Managing debt wisely is crucial to avoid financial stress and maintain good credit.

Summary: Why Debt is Important

Debt is an essential aspect of personal finance for several reasons:

1. **Investment in the Future:** Debt, like student loans or a mortgage, can enable you to invest in important life goals, such as education or homeownership.

2. **Financial Flexibility:** It can provide financial flexibility by allowing you to make purchases or investments when you don't have the cash upfront.

3. **Credit Building**: Responsible debt management helps you build a positive credit history and improve your credit score, which opens doors to better financial opportunities.

4. **Interest Costs:** Understanding interest rates and the cost of borrowing helps you make informed financial decisions and minimize the overall cost of debt.

5. **Risk of Overindebtedness**: Managing debt wisely is crucial to avoid excessive debt levels that can lead to financial stress and harm your credit score.

Closing Summary

Debt is a double-edged sword in the world of personal finance. When used wisely, it can be a valuable tool for achieving essential goals and managing your finances effectively. However, mishandling debt can lead to financial trouble and long-term consequences. As Emma realized, understanding the types of debt, interest rates, credit scores, and the importance of responsible borrowing is essential for making informed financial decisions. Remember, debt is a financial responsibility that should be approached with careful consideration and planning to ensure a prosperous financial future.

CHAPTER 3

Net Worth

Introduction to Net Worth

Welcome to the fascinating world of net worth, a crucial concept in the realm of personal finance. As you step into adulthood, understanding your net worth becomes an essential part of managing your financial well-being. In this chapter, we'll join Chris, an 18-year-old with dreams of financial success, on a journey to explore the concept of net worth.

Chapter: Chris's Quest for Financial Clarity

In the bustling town of Prosperville, Chris was a high school graduate excited about the prospect of independence. He had always been savvy about earning money, whether it was through part-time jobs, odd gigs, or selling homemade crafts. However, Chris realized that being financially responsible required more than just earning money—it was about knowing where that money was going and how it was growing.

One day, Chris stumbled upon the term "net worth" while browsing a financial website. It sounded intriguing, so he decided to delve into it further. Chris discovered that net worth was a way to measure their financial health. It was the difference between his assets and liabilities.

Fun Fact #1: Net worth = Assets - Liabilities

Assets, Chris learned, were things he owned, like savings, investments, a car, and even his collection of vintage comic books. On the flip side, liabilities were what he owed, such as student loans, credit card balances, and any outstanding debts.

Chris decided to calculate his own net worth. He listed all his assets and their estimated values. This included his savings account, the value of their car, and his growing investment portfolio from years of selling crafts and saving diligently. On the liabilities side, he included a student loan for college tuition and a small credit card balance from an impulsive shopping spree.

Fun Fact #2: Your net worth can be positive (assets > liabilities) or negative (liabilities > assets).

When Chris crunched the numbers, he found that his assets exceeded his liabilities. Chris had a positive net worth! This was a moment of pride and a realization that his financial efforts had paid off.

Chris decided to monitor his net worth regularly, updating it as his financial situation changed. He understood that his net worth could increase by paying down debts, saving more, or making wise investments. It could also decrease if he accumulated more liabilities or saw a drop in asset values.

Fun Fact #3: Your net worth can change over time as you make financial decisions.

Summary: Why Net Worth is Important

Understanding and tracking your net worth is essential for several reasons:

1. **Financial Health**: It provides a snapshot of your financial health, helping you assess whether you're making progress toward your financial goals.

2. **Progress Measurement**: Net worth serves as a benchmark to measure your financial progress over time. Watching it grow can be motivating and rewarding.

3. **Goal Setting**: It assists in setting financial goals. By knowing your current net worth, you can set realistic targets for the future.

4. **Budgeting Aid**: Monitoring your net worth can help you make informed decisions about your spending, saving, and investing.

5. **Debt Management**: It encourages responsible debt management by making you aware of your liabilities and their impact on your net worth.

Closing Summary

Net worth is your financial compass, guiding you on your journey to financial success. As Chris discovered, it's a powerful tool that helps you assess your financial health, set goals, and track your progress. Whether your net worth is positive or negative, it's a starting point for building wealth and achieving your dreams. Remember, your net worth isn't fixed; it can change as you make smart financial decisions. By regularly monitoring and working to increase it, you can pave the way for a more secure and prosperous financial future.

CHAPTER 4

Credit

Introduction to Credit

Welcome to the world of credit, a concept that becomes increasingly important as you step into adulthood. Credit can open doors to financial opportunities, but it's essential to understand how to use it wisely. In this chapter, we'll follow the journey of Mark, an 18-year-old eager to explore the world of credit and learn why it matters.

Chapter: Mark's Path to Credit Wisdom

In the vibrant city of Financetown, Mark was a high school graduate ready to take on the challenges of adulthood. He knew that managing his money effectively was crucial, but the idea of credit intrigued him. Mark had heard both positive and negative stories about credit, so he decided to dig deeper.

Mark discovered that credit was like a financial superpower. It allowed people to borrow money to make purchases or investments, even if they didn't have the cash upfront. This newfound knowledge led Mark to explore different forms of credit.

Fun Fact #1: Credit allows you to access money you don't have on hand.

Mark found that credit came in various forms, including credit cards, personal loans, and mortgages. Each had its purpose and terms. For instance, credit cards were handy for everyday spending and building a credit history, while personal loans could be used for various purposes like financing a vacation or consolidating debt.

Excited by the possibilities, Mark decided to apply for his first credit card. He learned that when using a credit card, you essentially borrowed money from the card issuer and promised to pay it back later. However, credit cards came with interest rates, and if you didn't pay off the balance in full each month, interest would accrue.

Fun Fact #2: Credit cards allow you to make purchases on credit, but you must pay off the balance to avoid interest charges.

Mark got his first credit card and began using it responsibly. He made small purchases and paid the balance in full each month to avoid interest charges. He soon realized that his responsible credit card use was helping him build a credit history.

Credit history, Mark learned, was like a report card for your financial behavior. It included information about your credit accounts, payment history, and any outstanding debts. Lenders and creditors used this information to determine whether to approve your applications for loans or credit cards and at what interest rates.

Fun Fact #3: Your credit history affects your ability to borrow money and the terms you'll receive.

As Mark continued his credit journey, he also became aware of the importance of credit scores. A credit score was a three-digit number that summarized his credit history. A higher score indicated better creditworthiness, making it easier to qualify for loans and credit cards with favorable terms.

Fun Fact #4: A higher credit score opens doors to better financial opportunities.

Mark realized that to maintain a good credit score, he needed to:

1. Pay bills on time.

2. Keep credit card balances low.

3. Avoid opening too many new accounts.

4. Monitor his credit report for errors.

Summary: Why Credit is Important

Credit is essential for several reasons:

1. **Access to Opportunities**: It allows you to access financial opportunities like loans and credit cards, helping you make purchases, pursue education, or buy a home.

2. **Credit History Building:** Responsible credit use helps you build a positive credit history, which is crucial for future borrowing.

3. **Interest Rates**: It impacts the interest rates you'll receive on loans and credit cards. Good credit can save you money on interest charges.

4. **Financial Flexibility**: Credit provides financial flexibility by allowing you to make purchases even when you don't have the cash upfront.

5. **Emergency Fund**: It can serve as a backup fund in emergencies when you need quick access to money.

Closing Summary

Credit is a powerful financial tool that can shape your financial future. As Mark discovered, responsible credit use can help you build a positive credit history, open doors to better financial opportunities, and even save you money on interest charges. However, it's essential to use credit wisely and monitor your credit history to maintain good creditworthiness. Whether you're using a credit card for everyday purchases or taking out a loan for a significant investment, understanding the world of credit is a crucial step toward achieving your financial goals in adulthood.

CHAPTER 5

Saving

Introduction to Saving

Welcome to the world of saving, a fundamental concept in personal finance that becomes increasingly important as you step into adulthood. Saving is the cornerstone of financial security and achieving your goals. In this chapter, we'll join Sarah, an 18-year-old with dreams of financial independence, as she embarks on a journey to explore the art of saving.

Chapter: Sarah's Path to Financial Freedom

In the vibrant town of Prosperityville, Sarah was a high school graduate ready to take control of her financial destiny. She had big dreams—attending college, traveling the world, and eventually buying her dream home. But she knew that making these dreams a reality required more than just earning money; it required the discipline of saving.

Sarah's saving adventure began with a simple piggy bank. She had heard the phrase "saving for a rainy day" and decided to put it into practice. Every time she received an allowance or earned money from her part-time job, she would drop some spare change into her trusty piggy bank.

Fun Fact #1: Saving for a rainy day means setting aside money for unexpected expenses or emergencies.

As time went on, Sarah's piggy bank grew heavier. She realized that saving money gave her a sense of financial security. If her car needed repairs or an unexpected medical bill popped up, she had a cushion to fall back on.

Sarah's interest in saving expanded beyond her piggy bank. She opened a savings account at a local bank, where she could deposit her money and earn a bit of interest. She learned that interest was like a reward for saving; the bank paid her for keeping her money with them.

Fun Fact #2: Banks pay you interest for keeping your money in a savings account.

Sarah also set specific savings goals. She wanted to save for a college fund, an epic backpacking trip across Europe, and eventually a down payment on a house. She realized that having concrete goals gave her motivation to save consistently.

Fun Fact #3: Setting savings goals helps you stay focused and motivated.

To make her savings grow faster, Sarah explored the power of compound interest. She discovered that compound interest allowed her to earn interest not only on her initial savings but also on the interest her savings had already earned.

Fun Fact #4: Compound interest can help your savings grow faster over time.

Sarah's journey wasn't always smooth. There were temptations to spend her savings on trendy gadgets or expensive dinners with friends. But she learned to distinguish between her needs and wants. She allowed herself some fun spending, but always made sure to prioritize her savings goals.

Summary: Why Saving is Important

Saving is vital for several reasons:

1. **Financial Security**: Saving provides a safety net for unexpected expenses or emergencies, ensuring you can cover unexpected bills without going into debt.

2. **Goal Achievement**: It allows you to work toward your dreams, whether it's going to college, traveling, or buying a home.

3. **Compound Interest**: Saving and investing early can lead to significant wealth growth over time, thanks to the power of compound interest.

4. **Peace of Mind**: Knowing you have money set aside for future needs or goals brings peace of mind and reduces financial stress.

5. **Financial Freedom**: Saving paves the way for financial independence, giving you the freedom to make choices that align with your values and goals.

Closing Summary

Saving is the key to financial security and achieving your dreams. As Sarah discovered, it's a simple but powerful concept that empowers you to take control of your financial future. Whether you're starting with a piggy bank or opening a savings account, the habit of saving is a journey that leads to greater financial freedom and the ability to turn your dreams into reality. Remember, every penny saved is a step closer to the life you want to live, and the earlier you start, the more significant the impact on your financial future. So, embrace the art of saving, set your goals, and watch your financial dreams come to life!

CHAPTER 6

Investing

Introduction to Investing

Welcome to the exciting world of investing, where your money has the potential to grow and work for you. As you step into adulthood, understanding the fundamentals of investing is a valuable skill. In this chapter, we'll follow the journey of Joe, an 18-year-old eager to explore the world of investing and discover why it matters.

Chapter: Joe's Adventure in Investing

In the bustling city of Prosperityville, Joe was a high school graduate with a bright future ahead. While most of his peers were eager to start their college journeys or careers, Joe was curious about something else—investing. He had heard stories of people who had turned small investments into significant wealth, and he wanted to learn how to do the same.

Joe's journey began with a simple question: "What is investing?" He soon found the answer. Investing meant using your money to buy assets like stocks, bonds, or real estate with the expectation of earning a profit over time. It was like planting a seed and watching it grow into a tree bearing fruit.

Fun Fact #1: Investing is like planting a financial seed that can grow over time.

To get started, Joe decided to explore the stock market, a place where people bought and sold shares of companies. He learned that by purchasing stocks, he were essentially becoming part-owners of those companies. If the companies did well and their stock prices increased, Joe could make a profit when he sold their shares.

Joe opened an investment account and began researching companies that he was interested in. He learned that it was essential to diversify his investments by spreading his money across different types of assets and industries. This reduced the risk of losing everything if one investment didn't perform well.

Fun Fact #2: Diversifying your investments helps spread risk and potentially increase returns.

As Joe started investing, he discovered the concept of risk and return. He learned that while some investments offered the potential for high returns, they also came with higher risks. Conversely, safer investments tended to have lower returns.

For example, investing in stocks could offer substantial returns over the long term, but it came with the risk of price fluctuations. On the other hand, investing in bonds was considered less risky, but the potential returns were lower.

Fun Fact #3: Understanding risk and return helps you make informed investment choices.

To grow his investments, Joe also explored the power of compounding. He realized that when he earned returns on his investments, those returns could earn even more returns in the future. It was like a snowball effect, where his money grew exponentially over time.

Fun Fact #4: Compounding can significantly increase your wealth over time.

Joe's investment journey was not without its challenges. He experienced market ups and downs, but He learned to stay calm and stick to his long-term investment strategy. He understood that investing was not about quick gains but about patience and discipline.

Summary: Why Investing is Important

Investing is crucial for several reasons:

1. **Wealth Building**: It offers the potential for your money to grow significantly over time, helping you achieve long-term financial goals.

2. **Financial Independence**: Investing can provide a source of passive income, allowing you to work toward financial independence and early retirement.

3. **Diversification**: It allows you to diversify your assets and spread risk, reducing the impact of poor-performing investments.

4. **Hedging Against Inflation**: Investing can help your money keep pace with or outpace inflation, preserving your purchasing power.

5. **Long-Term Goals**: It's essential for reaching long-term goals like buying a home, funding education, or retiring comfortably.

Closing Summary

Investing is the key to growing your wealth and achieving financial freedom. As Joe discovered, it's a journey that involves learning, patience, and discipline. Whether you're interested in stocks, bonds, real estate, or other investment options, the earlier you start, the more time your money has to grow. Remember, investing is not a get-rich-quick scheme; it's a path to building a secure financial future. So, embrace the world of investing, set your goals, and watch your financial dreams become a reality!

CHAPTER 7

Homeownership

Introduction to Homeownership

Welcome to the world of homeownership, a significant milestone in many adults' lives. As you step into adulthood, the idea of owning your own home may start to take shape. In this chapter, we'll follow the journey of Maya, an 18-year-old with dreams of owning a place to call her own, and explore why homeownership is an important financial goal.

Chapter: Maya's Quest for Her Dream Home

In the charming town of Dreamsville, Maya was an 18-year-old with a head full of dreams. While some of her friends were excited about starting college, Maya had a different vision—she wanted to own her own home. She had heard stories of the sense of security and accomplishment that came with homeownership, and she was determined to make it happen.

Maya began her journey by learning about the basics of homeownership. She discovered that owning a home meant that you were the sole owner of a piece of property, and you could live there or rent it out to others. It was like having a place to call your own in the world.

Fun Fact #1: Homeownership means you have complete control over your living space.

To understand the financial aspect, Maya decided to explore the concept of mortgages. A mortgage was like a loan specifically designed for buying a home. It allowed you to purchase a property, even if you didn't have the full purchase price upfront. However, she realized that getting a mortgage required a down payment—a substantial initial payment made when buying a home.

Maya learned that different types of homes were available, from cozy apartments to spacious houses. The type of home you chose often depended on your budget, lifestyle, and long-term plans. Some people preferred the convenience of an apartment, while others dreamed of a house with a big backyard.

Fun Fact #2: The type of home you choose depends on your preferences and budget.

Maya also discovered that owning a home came with responsibilities. Homeowners were responsible for maintenance, repairs, property taxes, and homeowners' insurance. It was a bit like taking care of a pet—there were ongoing costs and occasional surprises.

But the idea of homeownership was appealing to Maya for many reasons. She realized that owning a home could be a smart financial move. Unlike renting, where you paid someone else's mortgage, homeownership allowed you to build equity in your property. Equity was like a portion of the home that you owned outright. It grew over time as you paid down your mortgage and as the property's value increased.

Fun Fact #3: Homeownership builds equity, which can be a valuable asset.

As Maya continued her journey, she also learned about the potential for home appreciation. Home appreciation meant that over time, the value of your home could increase. This could be due to various factors like location, improvements, or market trends. It was like watching your investment grow.

Fun Fact #4: Home appreciation can increase the value of your investment.

Summary: Why Homeownership is Important

Homeownership is significant for several reasons:

1. **Ownership and Control**: It gives you complete control over your living space, allowing you to customize and decorate it as you wish.

2. **Financial Investment**: Homeownership builds equity, which is a valuable asset that can grow over time.

3. **Stability**: It provides stability and a sense of belonging, as you have a permanent place to call home.

4. **Long-Term Wealth**: Real estate has the potential for appreciation, allowing you to build long-term wealth.

5. **Tax Benefits**: Homeownership can offer tax benefits, such as deductions for mortgage interest and property taxes.

Closing Summary

Homeownership is one of the fastest and easiest ways to wealth. Homeownership is a significant financial goal that many adults aspire to achieve. As Maya's journey illustrates, it offers a sense of security, control, and the potential for long-term wealth. While it comes with responsibilities and upfront costs, the benefits of homeownership are undeniable. Whether you're dreaming of a cozy apartment or a spacious house, owning your own home can be a fulfilling and financially wise decision. So, embark on your homeownership journey, save for that down payment, and watch your dreams of having a place to call your own come true!

CHAPTER 8

Taxes

Introduction to Taxes

Welcome to the world of taxes, a topic that becomes increasingly relevant as you step into adulthood. Taxes are an essential part of our society, and understanding them is vital for responsible financial citizenship. In this chapter, we'll follow the journey of Jake, an 18-year-old ready to learn about taxes and why they matter.

Chapter: Jake's Tax Education

In the bustling town of Taxville, Jake was a recent high school graduate with big plans for the future. He was excited about starting his first job, but he had heard people talking about taxes and was curious about what it all meant. So, he decided to dive in and learn about the world of taxes.

Jake began by understanding the basics of taxes. He learned that taxes were mandatory financial contributions that individuals and businesses paid to the government. These funds were used to support various public services, such as education, healthcare, infrastructure, and social programs.

Fun Fact #1: Taxes fund essential government services that benefit society.

Jake's first paycheck was a bit of an eye-opener. He noticed that a portion of his earnings was deducted for taxes. This deduction was called income tax, and it was a percentage of his income that went to both federal and state governments. Jake learned that the amount of income tax he owed depended on his income level and various deductions or credits he might qualify for.

Fun Fact #2: Income tax is calculated based on your income and may vary depending on your circumstances.

As Jake explored further, he discovered that there were different types of taxes. In addition to income tax, there were payroll taxes (like Social Security and Medicare), sales tax (added to purchases), property tax (based on the value of real estate), and more. Each tax served a specific purpose and was collected differently.

For example, sales tax was added to the cost of most goods and services when purchased. Property tax was assessed annually based on the value of the property you owned. Jake realized that understanding these various taxes was essential for managing his finances effectively.

Fun Fact #3: Different types of taxes serve different purposes and are collected in various ways.

Jake also learned about the importance of filing a tax return. This was an annual process where individuals reported their income and calculated their tax liability. The government used this information to determine whether you owed additional taxes or were eligible for a tax refund.

Jake was pleasantly surprised to learn that tax refunds were possible. If you had too much tax withheld from your paycheck during the year, you could receive a refund when you filed your tax return. It was like getting a bonus check from the government.

Fun Fact #4: Filing a tax return can result in a tax refund if you've overpaid your taxes.

Summary: Why Taxes Are Important

Taxes are crucial for several reasons:

1. **Funding Government Services**: Taxes provide the government with the revenue needed to fund essential services like education, healthcare, and infrastructure.

2. **Income Redistribution**: They help redistribute income by supporting social programs that assist those in need.

3. **Maintaining Public Order**: Taxes are used to maintain law and order, including funding law enforcement and the judicial system.

4. **Economic Stabilization**: They can be used to influence economic behavior and promote economic stability.

5. **Civic Responsibility**: Paying taxes is a civic duty that supports the well-being of society.

Closing Summary

Taxes are an integral part of our financial lives, and understanding them is essential for responsible citizenship. As Jake discovered, taxes fund the services and programs that make our society function. While it can be challenging to see a portion of your hard-earned money go toward taxes, it's important to remember that taxes are an investment in our collective well-being. So, embrace your role as a responsible taxpayer, learn about the tax system, and use your knowledge to make informed financial decisions.

CHAPTER 9

Entrepreneurship

Introduction to Entrepreneurship

Welcome to the world of entrepreneurship, where individuals turn their ideas into businesses and embark on exciting journeys of innovation and success. As you step into adulthood, the concept of entrepreneurship may hold the promise of financial independence and creative fulfillment. In this chapter, we'll follow the story of Jacob, an 18-year-old with dreams of entrepreneurship, and explore why it's an important and empowering path.

Chapter: Jacob's Journey as an Entrepreneur

In the dynamic town of Innovationville, Jacob was an 18-year-old with a passion for problem-solving and a vision for making a difference. While many of his peers were exploring traditional career paths, Jacob was drawn to entrepreneurship—a path where individuals create their own businesses and forge their destinies.

Jacob's entrepreneurial journey began with an idea. He had observed a common problem among his friends—finding affordable and nutritious meals on a tight budget. Jacob decided to create a solution: a meal delivery service that provided healthy and affordable meals to college students.

Fun Fact #1: Entrepreneurship often starts with identifying a problem and finding a creative solution.

But starting a business wasn't as simple as having an idea. Jacob had to research the market, plan his business strategy, secure funding, and navigate the legal aspects of entrepreneurship. He realized that being an entrepreneur required a diverse set of skills and the determination to overcome challenges.

He decided to create a business plan, a roadmap outlining his business goals, target audience, marketing strategy, and financial projections. This plan would not only guide his efforts but also attract potential investors who believed in his vision.

Fun Fact #2: A well-thought-out business plan is essential for guiding your entrepreneurial journey and securing funding.

To turn his idea into reality, Jacob needed startup capital. He explored various options, from personal savings to seeking investors or applying for small business loans. Jacob learned that securing funding was often one of the most significant challenges for entrepreneurs, but it was a crucial step in launching a business.

With determination and a solid business plan in hand, Jacob launched his meal delivery service. It wasn't easy; there were late nights, marketing struggles, and unexpected setbacks. But Jacob's passion and resilience fueled his determination to succeed.

As his business grew, Jacob discovered the importance of marketing and branding. He realized that effective marketing strategies could help reach a wider audience and create a loyal customer base. Social media, word-of-mouth, and partnerships with local colleges became essential tools in his entrepreneurial toolkit.

Fun Fact #3: Marketing and branding are vital for attracting customers and building a strong business presence.

Jacob's journey as an entrepreneur was marked by both successes and failures. He learned that entrepreneurship was a path filled with uncertainty, but it also offered unparalleled opportunities for personal and financial growth. Jacob's business not only addressed a common problem but also created jobs and contributed to the local economy.

Summary: Why Entrepreneurship is Important

Entrepreneurship is significant for several reasons:

1. **Innovation**: Entrepreneurs drive innovation by creating new products, services, and solutions to address societal needs and challenges.

2. **Job Creation**: Small businesses and startups, often founded by entrepreneurs, are major sources of job creation and economic growth.

3. **Economic Empowerment**: Entrepreneurship empowers individuals to take control of their financial futures and pursue their passions.

4. **Problem Solving**: Entrepreneurs identify and solve real-world problems, leading to improved quality of life and convenience for consumers.

5. **Community Development**: Successful businesses contribute to the vitality and development of local communities.

Closing Summary

Entrepreneurship is a dynamic and rewarding journey that allows individuals to turn their ideas into reality. As Alex's story illustrates, it involves creativity, determination, and a willingness to overcome challenges. Whether you dream of starting a small business, launching a tech startup, or pursuing any other entrepreneurial endeavor, the path of entrepreneurship is a powerful way to make a difference, both in your life and in the world. So, embrace your entrepreneurial spirit, dare to innovate, and pave the way for a future filled with possibility and impact.

CHAPTER 10

Financial Ethics

Introduction to Financial Ethics

Welcome to the realm of financial ethics, where principles of honesty, integrity, and fairness guide the decisions and actions we take in the world of finance. As you navigate adulthood, understanding the importance of ethical financial behavior is crucial for building trust, making responsible choices, and contributing positively to society. In this chapter, we'll join the journey of Nina, an 18-year-old who learns the significance of financial ethics and its impact on her life.

Chapter: Nina's Lesson in Financial Ethics

In the vibrant town of Ethicalville, Nina was an 18-year-old who had just started her first job at a local bank. She was excited about earning her own money and managing her finances independently. However, on her very first day, her supervisor, Mr. Smith, emphasized the importance of financial ethics.

Nina wondered, "What are financial ethics, and why do they matter?"

Mr. Smith explained that financial ethics were a set of moral principles that guided our financial behavior. They were about making ethical choices, being honest and transparent, and treating others with respect and fairness in all financial transactions.

Fun Fact #1: Financial ethics involve making morally sound decisions in financial matters.

Nina's journey in understanding financial ethics began with a simple scenario. She was tasked with reviewing a loan application from a young couple, Amy and Ben. The couple had good credit scores and stable incomes, but their loan application contained some false information about their expenses.

Nina was torn between her job's pressure to approve the loan and her growing understanding of financial ethics. She realized that approving the loan based on false information would be unethical, as it could put the couple and the bank at risk.

Fun Fact #2: Financial ethics often involve making difficult decisions that align with moral principles.

Nina decided to consult with Mr. Smith, seeking guidance on how to handle the situation. Mr. Smith praised Nina's ethical dilemma recognition and encouraged her to follow the bank's policy of requiring accurate information for loan approval. Nina learned that making ethical choices might not always be easy, but it was the right thing to do.

As Nina continued her journey, she encountered other aspects of financial ethics. She learned about the importance of financial transparency, where individuals and organizations were open and honest about their financial activities. Transparency built trust and credibility in financial relationships.

Fun Fact #3: Financial transparency builds trust and credibility in financial interactions.

Nina also discovered the significance of fair and equitable treatment in financial matters. Discrimination based on race, gender, age, or other factors was unethical and illegal. Financial institutions were expected to treat all customers fairly and equally.

Fun Fact #4: Treating everyone with fairness and equality is a fundamental principle of financial ethics.

One day, Nina came across a news story about a company that had engaged in fraudulent financial practices, causing harm to investors and employees. The story highlighted the devastating consequences of unethical behavior in the financial world. Nina realized that financial ethics weren't just about following rules; they were about upholding moral values and preventing harm to others.

Summary: Why Financial Ethics Are Important

Financial ethics are essential for several reasons:

1. **Trust and Integrity**: They build trust and integrity in financial transactions, fostering healthy relationships between individuals, businesses, and institutions.

2. **Preventing Harm**: Ethical behavior prevents financial harm to individuals and society by discouraging fraud, deception, and unfair practices.

3. **Credibility**: Ethical financial behavior enhances the credibility and reputation of individuals and organizations, leading to better opportunities and success.

4. **Legal Compliance**: Many unethical financial practices are illegal, so adhering to financial ethics helps avoid legal consequences.

5. **Contributing to Society**: Ethical financial behavior contributes to the overall well-being of society by promoting fairness, transparency, and responsible financial decisions.

Closing Summary

Financial ethics are the moral compass that guides our financial decisions and actions. As Nina's journey illustrates, they are about making choices that align with honesty, integrity, and fairness. Understanding and practicing financial ethics isn't just a responsibility; it's an opportunity to build trust, credibility, and positive financial relationships. In a world where financial decisions have far-reaching consequences, embracing financial ethics is a powerful way to make a meaningful and ethical impact on your financial journey and the world around you.

CHAPTER 11

Funds

Introduction to Funds: Exploring Hedge Funds and Private Equity Funds

Welcome to the world of funds, where individuals and organizations pool their money together to invest in a variety of assets and opportunities. Funds are an essential part of the financial landscape, and understanding them is crucial as you navigate adulthood. In this chapter, we'll dive into the world of funds, with a focus on hedge funds and private equity funds, and explore their significance in the financial world.

Chapter: A Tale of Two Funds

In the bustling city of Financeville, Sue and Luke, both 18-year-olds, were keen to explore the world of finance and investments. They had heard about different types of funds and decided to learn more about two prominent ones: hedge funds and private equity funds.

Part 1: The World of Hedge Funds

Sue's curiosity led her to the world of hedge funds. She learned that hedge funds were investment vehicles that pooled money from various investors, including high-net-worth individuals and institutions. These funds were managed by skilled professionals known as fund managers.

Fun Fact #1: Hedge funds are managed by financial experts who aim to maximize returns for investors.

Sue was intrigued by the flexibility of hedge funds. Unlike traditional investments like stocks or bonds, hedge funds had the freedom to invest in a wide range of assets, from stocks and bonds to real estate, currencies, and even derivatives. This flexibility allowed hedge fund managers to adapt to different market conditions and potentially generate significant returns.

Fun Fact #2: Hedge funds have a broader investment mandate than traditional investments.

Sue also discovered the concept of hedge fund strategies. Hedge funds employed various strategies to achieve their financial goals, such as long/short equity, event-driven, or macro strategies. Each strategy had its unique approach to investing and risk management.

For instance, a long/short equity hedge fund might buy stocks they believe will increase in value (going long) while simultaneously selling stocks they believe will decline (going short). This strategy aimed to profit from both rising and falling markets.

Fun Fact #3: Hedge funds use different strategies to achieve their financial objectives.

Part 2: The World of Private Equity Funds

Meanwhile, Luke was drawn to the world of private equity funds. He discovered that private equity funds were investment funds that focused on acquiring, investing in, or providing financing for private companies. These funds often targeted businesses with growth potential.

Fun Fact #4: Private equity funds invest in privately held companies.

Luke found the process of private equity investments fascinating. Private equity funds typically acquired a significant stake in a company, often taking an active role in its management and decision-making. This involvement allowed private equity investors to influence the company's direction and potentially enhance its value.

Private equity investments were often long-term in nature, with the goal of improving the company's financial performance and eventually selling it at a profit. Luke learned that this approach required patience and a thorough understanding of the businesses they invested in.

Fun Fact #5: Private equity investors play an active role in the companies they invest in to enhance their value.

Summary: Why Funds Are Important

Funds, including hedge funds and private equity funds, play vital roles in the financial world for several reasons:

1. **Diversification**: Funds allow investors to diversify their portfolios by investing in a variety of assets or companies, reducing risk.

2. **Expert Management**: Skilled fund managers make investment decisions on behalf of investors, potentially maximizing returns.

3. **Access to Unique Opportunities**: Funds provide access to investment opportunities, strategies, and asset classes that may not be available to individual investors.

4. **Capital Allocation**: Funds allocate capital efficiently, directing money to where it's needed most, whether for business growth (private equity) or various investment opportunities (hedge funds).

5. **Risk Management**: Funds often employ risk management strategies to protect investors' capital and navigate volatile markets.

Closing Summary

Funds, whether hedge funds or private equity funds, are powerful tools in the financial world. They offer investors the opportunity to access a wide range of investments and strategies while benefiting from professional management. Understanding these funds is essential as you make financial decisions and consider investment opportunities. While they come with their own complexities and risks, funds have the potential to play a significant role in your financial journey, helping you achieve your goals and navigate the ever-evolving landscape of finance.

CLOSING

Closing: Embracing Financial Literacy for a New Life

As we conclude this journey through the fascinating world of financial literacy, it's important to reflect on why becoming financially literate is the perfect way to start a new life as an adult. The knowledge and skills you've gained in these chapters hold the key to unlocking a brighter and more secure future.

Financial literacy is not just about balancing budgets or understanding investment strategies; it's about empowerment. It empowers you to take control of your financial destiny, make informed decisions, and navigate the complex financial landscape with confidence.

Imagine a life where you have the knowledge to:

1. **Secure Your Future**: Financial literacy equips you with the tools to plan for the future, whether that means buying a home, funding your education, or retiring comfortably. It allows you to set achievable goals and work towards them methodically.

2. **Protect Your Hard-Earned Money**: With financial literacy, you can safeguard your earnings by recognizing and avoiding scams, fraudulent schemes, and unnecessary fees. You become a vigilant guardian of your financial well-being.

3. **Invest in Yourself**: Understanding the principles of saving and investing ensures that your money works for you, creating opportunities for growth and financial freedom. You can aspire to achieve your dreams, whether they involve starting a business, traveling the world, or pursuing your passions.

4. **Navigate Life's Challenges**: Financial literacy provides a safety net during challenging times. You're better prepared to handle unexpected emergencies, job loss, or medical expenses without falling into financial despair.

5. **Contribute to Society**: As a financially literate individual, you have the capacity to give back and make a positive impact on your community. Whether through charitable donations, mentoring, or supporting local businesses, your financial stability can extend to benefit others.

6. **Achieve Peace of Mind**: Perhaps most importantly, financial literacy brings peace of mind. It reduces anxiety about money, minimizes financial stress, and enables you to focus on what truly matters in life—your relationships, personal growth, and well-being.

In a world where financial decisions are part of our daily lives, from managing expenses to planning for retirement, financial literacy is the ultimate life skill. It empowers you to make choices aligned with your values and aspirations, rather than being driven by financial pressures or ignorance.

Your journey towards financial literacy is ongoing. It involves continuous learning, adaptation to changing circumstances, and the willingness to seek guidance when needed. Remember that everyone's financial path is unique, and it's okay to make mistakes along the way. Each lesson learned is a stepping stone towards a more secure and prosperous future.

So, as you embark on this new phase of your life as an adult, embrace financial literacy as your faithful companion. It will guide you through the twists and turns of the financial world, helping you build a life of resilience, prosperity, and fulfillment. Embrace the power of financial literacy, and let it be your beacon towards a brighter, more promising future. Thank You for taking time to read this book! I wish you well on your financial future!